Who Was

Roberto Clemente?

Who Was
Roberto Clemente?

By James Buckley Jr.
Illustrated by Ted Hammond

Grosset & Dunlap
An Imprint of Penguin Group (USA) LLC

For Bill Pintard and the Santa Barbara Foresters, who are champions both on and off the field—JB

To my sister Robin—TH

GROSSET & DUNLAP
Published by the Penguin Group
Penguin Group (USA) LLC, 375 Hudson Street, New York, New York 10014, USA

USA | Canada | UK | Ireland | Australia | New Zealand | India | South Africa | China

penguin.com
A Penguin Random House Company

Text copyright © 2014 by James Buckley Jr. Illustrations copyright © 2014 by Ted Hammond. Cover illustration copyright © 2014 by Nancy Harrison. All rights reserved. Published by Grosset & Dunlap, a division of Penguin Young Readers Group, 345 Hudson Street, New York, New York 10014. GROSSET & DUNLAP is a trademark of Penguin Group (USA) LLC. Printed in the USA.

Library of Congress Cataloging-in-Publication Data is available.

ISBN 978-0-448-47961-3   10 9 8 7 6 5 4 3

Contents

Who Was
Roberto Clemente?

On a sunny autumn day in Puerto Rico in
1952, Roberto Clemente arrived at a ball field
wearing beat-up baseball pants. The eighteen-
year-old was carrying his old glove and wore a cap
with a long bill. The field was mostly dirt. The
baseballs there were used and scuffed. But that

didn't matter to the seventy or so young players who had showed up that day. All of them had the same goal: to be discovered by a scout from a Major League Baseball team. That year, sixteen teams based in the United States made up the majors, eight each in the American and National Leagues. For young ballplayers like Roberto, making the majors would be a dream come true.

Over the next few hours, Roberto did his best to realize that dream. He fired long, perfect throws from the outfield. He whizzed around the bases faster than any other player there. He ran a sixty-yard dash in 6.4 seconds (coming very close to the world record at the time—6.1 seconds!). And he hit line drive after line drive. After watching Roberto's performance, it was clear to the scouts that he had the skills to one day make the major leagues. One scout for the Brooklyn Dodgers said Roberto was the "greatest natural athlete I have ever seen."

A year later, his major league dream came true. He signed with the Brooklyn Dodgers and went on to have one of baseball's most remarkable careers. He worked hard to make the dreams of thousands of other people come true, too.

Chapter 1
A Guava-Branch Bat

In a town called Carolina, on the northeast corner of the island of Puerto Rico, Roberto Clemente Walker was born on August 18, 1934. Like many people from the island, he took the last names of both his mother and father. Throughout his life, however, Roberto was known by his father's last name, Clemente.

His parents, Melchor and Luisa, had five children. Roberto was the youngest. Sadly, his older sister, Anairis, died when Roberto was very young. She was burned in a kitchen accident and never recovered from her injuries.

But Roberto still had three older brothers. He also had a stepbrother and stepsister, Luisa's children from her first marriage. With a family

that big, there was always someone to play with.
And what they played was baseball.

"I loved baseball more than anything," Roberto
said later in life. "We played all day and wouldn't
care if we missed lunch. We played until it was
too dark to see."

Roberto earned a lifelong family nickname in these years. He did not like to be rushed and often said *"Momentito, momentito,"* which means "just a moment." His friends and family came to call him "Momen."

Momen and his friends and brothers played baseball after school and on weekends. They did not have formal teams and made up their own rules. They made their own gear. Roberto formed baseballs by wrapping old socks or rags very tightly with string and then sewing a piece of cloth over the socks. The boys carved baseball bats from the branches of guava trees. They sometimes hit crushed tin cans. For gloves, they sewed together old coffee sacks.

PUERTO RICO: PART OF THE USA

San Juan
Carolina
Puerto Rico
Ponce

THE COMMONWEALTH OF PUERTO RICO IS AN ISLAND TERRITORY OF THE UNITED STATES. THAT MEANS IT IS OWNED BY THE UNITED STATES, BUT IS NOT A STATE. JUAN PONCE DE LÉON FOUNDED THE FIRST EUROPEAN SETTLEMENT ON PUERTO RICO (SPANISH FOR "RICH PORT"), ESTABLISHING IT AS A SPANISH COLONY. IT HAS BEEN A COMMONWEALTH OF THE UNITED STATES SINCE 1952.

MOST OF ITS PEOPLE SPEAK SPANISH. PUERTO RICANS ARE AMERICAN CITIZENS BUT CANNOT VOTE IN NATIONAL ELECTIONS. ABOUT FOUR MILLION PEOPLE LIVE IN PUERTO RICO TODAY, BUT MORE THAN FIVE MILLION PEOPLE OF PUERTO RICAN DESCENT LIVE ON THE US MAINLAND.

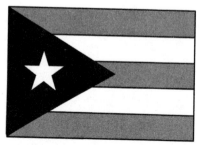

Luisa Walker loved her son, but she worried that he was focusing too much on baseball. "There were times he was so much in love with baseball that he didn't even care for food," she said. In fact, she once tried to burn his bat—but Roberto rescued it from the flames!

All this playing soon helped Roberto become one of the best young baseball players in Carolina. In a scrapbook of memories, he wrote about a seven-and-a-half-hour game in which he hit ten home runs. He was growing up strong and fast and could throw a baseball harder and farther than anyone else around. He watched a lot of baseball, too. To go to a game, his father gave him twenty-five cents. A game ticket was fifteen cents and the round-trip bus fare was a dime.

In the winter, the weather in Puerto Rico was still nice. Top players from the United States often came down to play in Puerto Rico's own professional league. It was a way for them to stay in shape during their off-season. Roberto watched those teams, including his favorite team, the San Juan Senadores. The Senadores played in the island's capital, San Juan, not far from Carolina.

Along with baseball, family was the most
important thing in young Roberto's life. His
family spent most evenings together, telling stories

or listening to the radio. His brother Justino remembered that they were the first family they knew with a radio. The Clementes were not poor, but they were far from rich. His father, Melchor, worked in a sugar factory and his mother, Luisa, did laundry for neighbors. Roberto and his brothers sometimes earned money by bringing water to the men working in the sugarcane fields. And Luisa ran a small market in the front of their house to bring in a bit more money.

Roberto became known as a boy who was always willing to help out. When he was eleven, Roberto went to a school that had no fence around it. He wanted to protect his school and the students. So Roberto rallied friends and neighbors to raise money to build the fence. When he was twelve, Roberto helped pull an injured person from a fiery car accident. He had to run across a highway to reach the crash!

When he was fourteen, Roberto was spotted by Roberto Marín, who ran a softball team for a local rice company. Most of the team's players were older. They were men with jobs who played the

game after work and on weekends. Marín believed Roberto could play with them. In 1948, when Roberto joined the Sello Rojo Rice factory team, he took his first big step into his baseball future.

Chapter 2
Here Come the Crabbers!

Although Roberto was a star shortstop for the adult baseball team Sello Rojo (which means "Red Seal"), at school, he used his powerful throwing arm to help the track team. He was so good at throwing the javelin that he even had a shot at the Olympics! But by his senior year, he chose to stick with baseball and left the javelin behind.

While still in high school, Roberto advanced in baseball to eventually join the Santurce Cangrejeros, whose name means "Crabbers." Santurce played in the top Puerto Rican pro baseball league. These men played baseball for their living. The team was run by Pedro Zorrilla, a man who would come to be known as "Mr. Baseball" in Puerto Rico. In the fall of 1952, he gave Roberto forty dollars a week to play for his team.

CARIBBEAN BASEBALL

BASEBALL WAS BROUGHT TO THE CARIBBEAN ISLANDS AS EARLY AS THE 1860S BY VISITING SAILORS, WHO PRACTICED "AMERICA'S PASTIME" WHEREVER THEY TRAVELED. ON THE ISLANDS, THOUSANDS OF YOUNG MEN TOOK UP THE SPORT.

BASEBALL HAS CONTINUED TO BE VERY POPULAR IN MANY CARIBBEAN COUNTRIES. THE DOMINICAN REPUBLIC HAS SENT HUNDREDS OF PLAYERS TO THE MAJOR LEAGUES IN RECENT DECADES.

ROBERTO CLEMENTE WAS ONE OF MORE THAN TWO HUNDRED BIG-LEAGUE PLAYERS WHO HAVE COME FROM PUERTO RICO. CUBA HAS WON OLYMPIC GOLD MEDALS IN BASEBALL AND OTHER INTERNATIONAL BASEBALL TOURNAMENTS. AND MEXICO AND VENEZUELA, TWO COUNTRIES THAT BORDER THE CARIBBEAN SEA, HAVE POPULAR BASEBALL LEAGUES.

MANY OF THE ISLANDS HAVE ACTIVE PRO LEAGUES TODAY. EACH WINTER SINCE 1949, A CARIBBEAN SERIES HAS BEEN HELD. THE CHAMPION TEAMS FROM FOUR AREAS—MEXICO, VENEZUELA, PUERTO RICO, AND THE DOMINICAN REPUBLIC—COMPETE TO WIN THAT SERIES.

The Crabbers included many top players from Puerto Rico and the United States. Some played or had played in the major leagues. The manager was Buster Clarkson, who had had been an infielder in the Negro leagues in the United States. He played a big part in helping Roberto improve his game. Roberto said that Buster "used to tell me I am as good as anybody in the big leagues. That helped me a lot."

Less than a month after debuting with the Crabbers, Roberto went to a major-league tryout. He threw harder and ran faster than any of the other young players. He was so impressive that several teams wanted to sign him up. However, he was still in high school. For Roberto and the scouts who were there that day, the tryout was only a sign of things to come.

In the winter of 1953–1954, after Roberto had finished high school, he was old enough to go after his biggest goal: signing with a major league team. Puerto Rico's pro teams were good, but the major leagues in the United States were the top of the baseball world. The scouts had watched him play for the Crabbers. Several big-league clubs offered him contracts. On Roberto's behalf, his father, Melchor, accepted a deal from the Brooklyn Dodgers, who played in New York City. Roberto was given a bonus of $10,000 for his first season,

which would begin in the spring of 1954. Soon after, the Milwaukee Braves offered him $30,000, but Roberto stuck with Brooklyn. He could have turned down the Dodgers' lower offer, but, as he said later, "It was hard, but I said I gave the Dodgers my word." For Roberto, keeping his promise was more important than any amount of money.

Roberto's next stop was not Brooklyn, however. It was in far-off Canada.

Chapter 3
Far-off Montreal

The Brooklyn Dodgers sent some of their younger players to Canada's Montreal Royals to improve and prepare for the major leagues. The Royals were part of the Dodgers' minor leagues—teams set up to develop future big-league talent. The Dodgers knew Roberto was good, but they also knew he wasn't completely ready yet.

Roberto got off to a great start with the Royals. In his first minor-league spring training game, he had hit an inside-the-park home run!

But life was hard in Montreal. He was a long way from home, and he was very lonely. It was much colder in Canada than in tropical Puerto Rico. Many people in Montreal spoke only French, while Roberto spoke Spanish and very little English.

To make matters worse, his teammates only spoke English! An older player from Cuba named Chico Fernández, who had been in the minors for several years, taught Roberto how to order "ham and eggs" in English for breakfast. At least he would not go hungry!

For the first time in his life, Roberto was forced to deal with segregation. Segregation means that people are kept separate—at restaurants, in hotels, in movie theaters, even at drinking fountains—according to the color of their skin. Though he was Puerto Rican, to people outside his island home, he was black. Canada was tolerant of all races. But in the 1950s in many parts of the United States, black people were considered second-class citizens. During a trip with the Royals to Richmond, Virginia, for example, Roberto and other black players were told they could not eat at a restaurant with their white teammates. They had to take their meals at a restaurant that was for blacks only.

This was upsetting to Roberto, especially because back home in Puerto Rico, segregation did not exist. "I don't believe in color," he later said. "I believe in people."

Roberto did not play often in Montreal. He would have a good game and then sit out several games in a row. Sometimes, his coach would substitute a pinch hitter even when Roberto knew he could drive in runs.

He became very confused and wondered why he wasn't playing every game and why the team wasn't making better use of his skills. Roberto told his brother Justino he was thinking of coming home.

"I never thought I would reach such heights," Roberto said later. "Then I did . . . and they wouldn't let me play."

In fact, the Dodgers had a plan . . . to hide Roberto!

Because Roberto had been signed to a one-year contract with Montreal, at the end of the year he would be eligible to be drafted by another team under the rules of Major League Baseball at that time. The Dodgers thought playing in the minors would give Roberto a chance to get even better. The next season, the Dodgers hoped to bring him up to the majors. In the meantime, they were hoping no one would find their gem—Roberto— in the minor leagues in Canada.

When the Royals' season was over, Roberto
returned home to Puerto Rico to live with his
family. He also rejoined the Santurce Crabbers
and helped them win the league championship.
Roberto played left field. The center fielder that
season was the great Willie Mays. Mays was
already a World Series hero for the New York

Giants and would go on to hit 660 homers in his Hall of Fame career. Like many major leaguers, Mays often played in Puerto Rico during the winter months, when Major League Baseball was not in season. The Crabbers went on to win the 1955 Caribbean Series and are still considered one of the best teams ever to play in Puerto Rico.

The news was not all good for Roberto during the Crabbers' season. On his way to visit his stepbrother Luis in the hospital, another driver hit the car Roberto was driving. Roberto hurt his neck and back, but he did not get medical help at the time. Luis passed away after the next day, and Roberto would suffer from his injuries for the rest of his life.

In November of that same year, a baseball meeting held in New York City changed Roberto's life in more positive way. Roberto Clemente's talent was too big to hide, even in Canada. The Dodgers' secret was out, and Roberto was now eligible to be drafted by another team. At the meeting, the Pittsburgh Pirates chose Roberto. Momen had made it to the major leagues for real this time.

Chapter 4
Welcome to the Bigs

Each year baseball teams prepare for the season at spring training. They work out and practice their skills. For young players, it's also a chance to demonstrate their skills. For Roberto, it was just another strange place to get used to.

Though Roberto had seen segregation in his time with the Royals, spring training with the Pirates in Florida was much worse. The team trained in Fort Myers. The white Pirates players stayed in a fancy hotel.

The black players stayed across town in homes owned by black people. They were not allowed in the nice hotel. White players enjoyed trips to golf clubs and swimming pools; black players were not invited. Even at the ballpark, there was segregation.

There were separate sections for black and white fans. There were even separate water fountains!

This separation of the races was still shocking to Roberto. There were black and white people in Puerto Rico, but they were not separate.

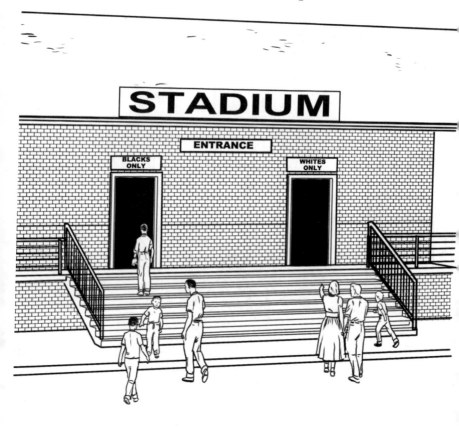

Back in Pennsylvania, it was difficult for Roberto to get to know his new teammates on the Pittsburgh Pirates since he did not speak English very well. "Not to speak the language," he said later. "That is a terrible problem. [It] meant you were different."

He told one writer, "I didn't even know where Pittsburgh was."

In the early 1950s, the Pirates were not a very good team. They had not been to the World Series since 1927. They had not had a winning season since 1948.

Roberto got into his first major league regular-season game on April 17, 1955. It was against the Brooklyn Dodgers, the team that had originally signed him! In his first at bat, he got his first career hit, an infield single. The Dodgers probably wondered if they had made a mistake by trying to hide Roberto in the minors rather than bringing him right up! For the next several months,

he did very well, hitting over .300. As the summer wore on, however, his hitting numbers started to slide. One reason was that he was lonely.

Roberto still missed his family and friends back in Puerto Rico. He didn't fit in with the American black players because he spoke little English. And he didn't fit in with most white players, either. His closest friends that year were the Garlands, a black couple with whom he roomed. They introduced Roberto to their friends, cooked dinner for him,

and helped him to feel more comfortable in his new surroundings.

Roberto missed a few games that season when his back was sore. It still bothered him after the car accident. Then and now, baseball players are expected to be tough and to "play through" minor injuries. When he asked for time off or talked about his injuries, he was sometimes ridiculed by other players, including his teammates. They wondered if he was faking his injuries or exaggerating them. And they didn't like complainers.

When the 1955 season was over, Roberto again headed home to Puerto Rico for the winter. The Pirates were pleased with his performance that season, but knew he could do better. "I would say that it was obvious that he had not played much professional baseball, that he had things to learn," Pirates president Joe Brown said. "But it was even more obvious that he had great talent."

SPRING TRAINING

MAJOR LEAGUE TEAMS HAVE HAD SPRING TRAINING SINCE THE 1920S, AND SOME AS FAR BACK AS THE 1880S. IN THOSE DAYS, MOST TEAMS WERE FROM THE NORTHEAST AND MIDWEST. IN LATE WINTER AND EARLY SPRING, IT WAS TOO COLD TO PRACTICE BASEBALL, SO THE TEAMS HEADED SOUTH TO PLAY IN THE WARMER WEATHER.

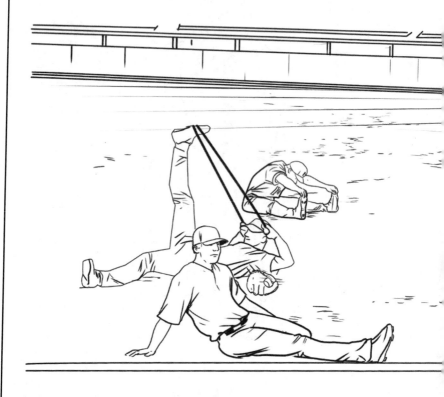

TODAY, TEAMS HAVE SPRING TRAINING FIELDS IN FLORIDA AND ARIZONA. THERE, THEY CAN GET IN SHAPE FOR THE COMING SEASON AND TRY OUT YOUNGER PLAYERS. THE PLAYERS STAY TOGETHER AND GET TO KNOW ONE ANOTHER. THE COACHES WATCH CAREFULLY TO SEE WHICH PLAYERS HAVE THE BEST SKILLS AND THEN DECIDE WHO WILL PLAY IN THE MAJOR LEAGUES AND WHO WILL STAY IN THE MINORS.

Chapter 5
Home and Away

Roberto spent the next several years that way—playing in Pittsburgh in the summer and then living and playing in Puerto Rico in the winter.

Slowly Roberto became more comfortable in Pittsburgh. Little by little, his English improved. However, sports reporters still had trouble speaking with him.

Some of the reporters were not kind to Roberto. They wrote down what he said in a way that made him sound uneducated. When he said "hit," they wrote "heet." When he said "big leagues," they wrote "beeg leegs." The way they wrote made fun of his heavy Spanish accent.

Then in 1957, his official baseball card printed his name as "Bob" Clemente, not Roberto. The mistake would be repeated for several more years. For a man with such pride in his heritage, this was a great insult. Because of such treatment,

BOB Clemente
PITTSBURGH PIRATES OUTFIELD

Roberto became determined to turn the fire that burned inside him into success on the ball field.

Roberto didn't hit many home runs, but stroked line-drive hits into the outfield. On defense, he was outstanding. He showed time and again why he had the best throwing arm in the sport.

BASEBALL CARDS

BASEBALL CARDS WERE FIRST PRINTED IN THE 1880S. THEY WERE INCLUDED IN PACKAGES OF TOBACCO. IN THE 1930S, CHEWING GUM COMPANIES STARTED SELLING CARDS WITH THEIR GUM. IN 1952, THE TOPPS CHEWING GUM COMPANY PRODUCED THE FIRST FULL SET OF MAJOR LEAGUE BASEBALL CARDS. THE TOPPS CARDS MADE COLLECTING A POPULAR HOBBY THAT CONTINUES TO THIS DAY.

PLAYER PHOTOS FOR THE CARDS ARE USUALLY TAKEN DURING SPRING TRAINING.

THE CARDS INCLUDE STATISTICS AND FACTS ABOUT THE PLAYERS, FACSIMILE AUTOGRAPHS, AND TEAM LOGOS. A NEW CARD DESIGN IS USED EACH YEAR.

IN THE 1980S, SEVERAL OTHER COMPANIES JOINED TOPPS IN MAKING BASEBALL CARDS. THE VALUE OF SOME OF THE MUCH OLDER CARDS ROSE DRAMATICALLY. IN 1991, A 1909 CARD OF HALL OF FAMER HONUS WAGNER WAS WORTH $451,000. BY 2011, THE SAME CARD HAD SOLD FOR $2.8 MILLION.

Meanwhile, when he played back home in the Puerto Rican league, he encouraged younger ballplayers and helped support his family with the money he was making on the baseball diamond. He bought his parents a home. He helped his brothers and his nieces and nephews, too.

In late 1958, Roberto took a break from baseball and went to South Carolina to train with the United States Marines.

In those days, all healthy young American men, including those from Puerto Rico, had to serve some time in the military. Roberto signed up for the Marine Reserves. After his training was over in early 1959, he was a Marine, but he would only have to serve in case of a war. After training for the Marines, it was back to baseball.

By 1960, after five seasons in the Major Leagues, Roberto was still not a star. He knew that he had to step up his game to make himself—and the Pirates—into winners.

Chapter 6
1960

Roberto got off to a great start in the 1960 season. In the first four months, he was among the best hitters in the league, and was driving in

more runs than ever. He was the National League (N.L.) Player of the Month for May. In July, Roberto was named to the N.L. All-Star team for the first time. The Pirates were doing very well, too, which was a big change from recent seasons.

As the summer continued, more and more people saw what his teammates already knew: Roberto Clemente was now one of the top outfielders in baseball. Roberto ended up the season with his best batting average yet and fourth-best in the N.L.

He also led the Pirates with ninety-four runs batted in and set a new career high with sixteen home runs. On September 25 the Pirates clinched the N.L. championship. That put them in the World Series for the first time in thirty-three years.

Luisa Clemente and Roberto's brother Matino flew up to Pittsburgh to watch Roberto play in the World Series. Roberto's father, Melchor, was afraid of flying. He stayed home in Carolina and listened to his son's games on the radio.

Along with baseball fans everywhere, Melchor heard one of the most exciting World Series ever. The powerful New York Yankees, the American League champions, boasted a lineup of sluggers including Mickey Mantle, Yogi Berra, and Roger Maris. In one World Series game, they beat Pittsburgh 16–3 and in another 12–0. After six games, the Pirates had scored seventeen runs, while the Yankees had piled up forty-six! However, the Pirates managed to win three games.

The seventh game would decide it all.

Roberto had at least one hit in each of the first six games. He played spectacular defense, making several key throws.

Game seven of the 1960 World Series was one
of the most memorable ever. The Pirates trailed 7–4
going into the bottom of the eighth inning. But
they rallied to score five runs to take a 9–7 lead!

THE WORLD SERIES

THE WORLD SERIES IS USUALLY PLAYED IN LATE OCTOBER, AT THE END OF THE REGULAR MAJOR LEAGUE BASEBALL SEASON. IT IS A SEVEN-GAME SERIES BETWEEN THE CHAMPIONS OF THE AMERICAN LEAGUE AND THE NATIONAL LEAGUE. THE FIRST TEAM TO WIN FOUR GAMES IS THE WORLD SERIES CHAMPION.

THE FIRST WORLD SERIES WAS PLAYED IN 1903 BETWEEN THE BOSTON AMERICANS (LATER CALLED THE RED SOX) AND THE PITTSBURGH PIRATES (BOSTON WON). THE WORLD SERIES HAS BEEN PLAYED EVERY YEAR SINCE, EXCEPT 1904, WHEN THE NEW YORK GIANTS REFUSED TO PLAY, AND 1994, WHEN ALL MAJOR LEAGUE PLAYERS WERE ON STRIKE. OVER THE PAST 110 YEARS, THE NEW YORK YANKEES HAVE WON TWENTY-SEVEN WORLD SERIES, THE MOST BY ANY TEAM.

Roberto knocked in one run in the rally and scored another. Then the Yankees came back to tie the score in the top of the ninth.

The first batter of the bottom of the ninth was Pirates second baseman Bill Mazeroski. He hit a home run to left field to make the Pirates the winners, 10–9! It was the first time that a last-inning home run had ever won a World Series! Pittsburgh fans celebrated into the night.

For the first time since coming to the United States, Roberto was a baseball champion. He was very happy to share the win with his teammates and with his family.

But after the season was over, the 1960 N.L. Most Valuable Player was announced after voting by a national group of baseball writers. The winner was Roberto's teammate, shortstop Dick Groat.

Roberto finished eighth, even though he felt he had had a better season than several of the players who finished ahead of him. He was very hurt by not being selected higher. He felt that the writers who had voted for the award had not voted for him because of his race and because of his trouble with English. Roberto had never really connected with most of the men who wrote about the team.

However, he had connected with the Pittsburgh fans. "[My] biggest thrill was when I come out of the clubhouse after the last Series game and saw thousands of fans in the street," he said.

"I did not feel like a player at the time. I [felt] like one of those [people], and I walked the streets among them."

Back home in Puerto Rico, he was greeted as a hero. But he always remembered how that MVP vote had made him feel.

Chapter 7
Honors and Marriage

As good as he was on the field, Roberto was still facing racism off it. At this time in America, the question of civil rights—equal rights for people of all races—was a major issue. He was not afraid to speak about his feelings.

During spring training before the 1961 season, he and other black teammates still lived apart from the white players. Roberto said, "In a way it was like being in prison. Everybody else on the team has fun during spring training. They swim, play golf, and go to the beaches. The only thing we can do is put in time until we head north. It's no fun."

Roberto watched the news about the civil rights movement closely.

He greatly admired its leader, Dr. Martin Luther King Jr. Dr. King later visited Puerto Rico and spent time with Roberto and his family.

But Roberto soon turned his focus back to the ball field. In 1961, Roberto was the top hitter in the National League. His batting average of .351 was better than any other N.L. player. Along with improving his hitting, Roberto continued to be a fantastic right fielder. After the 1961 season, he won the Gold Glove, given to players for fielding excellence. Players and coaches vote to choose the best player at each position in each league. Roberto would go on to win the Gold Glove award every season after that. His career total of twelve Gold Gloves is still tied for most all-time among outfielders with Willie Mays, his former teammate on the Crabbers.

After the 1961 season, Roberto was given a silver bat trophy for his batting title. When he returned home later to Puerto Rico, he said, "In the name of my family, in the name of Puerto Rico, and in the name of all the players who didn't have a chance to play for Puerto Rico in the big leagues, I thank you."

ROBERTO CLEMENTE

Whenever he could, Roberto talked about Puerto Rico. He was enormously proud of his island home. He returned there every autumn throughout his career.

He was thankful to the older players who had helped him learn the game, and he spent as much time as he could helping younger players improve their skills.

In early 1964, while in Puerto Rico, Roberto met a young woman named Vera Zabala at a drugstore and quickly fell in love. He pursued her with the same passion that he showed on the baseball field.

Vera Zabala was twenty-two years old and had a job at a bank. When Roberto introduced himself, she was polite, but that was all. She knew he was one of the most famous people on the island—but she was not a baseball fan. Over the next several months, Roberto asked her out again and again. He visited her at the bank and sent her letters. Eventually, Roberto won her over. She agreed to date him, but only after getting permission from her parents.

On the day of their first date, Roberto picked
her up at the bank. Vera's coworkers were so
excited to see the baseball star, they all came out
to the street to watch the couple leave!

Roberto was in a hurry. "The first time he
came to my home, Roberto said he was going to
marry me," Vera remembered. "A few dates later,
he brought pictures of houses. He also brought a
diamond ring."

He soon went to Vera's father and asked if he could marry her. Mr. Zabala was afraid that Roberto was a big star who would want to date many other women. "I can walk down to the corner and probably get ten girls," Roberto told him. "But I don't care. The woman I love is here."

Roberto and Vera were married on November 14, 1964.

Chapter 8
Family First

Along with his success on the baseball field, Roberto now had something else to be proud of—his growing family. Roberto and Vera had their first son, Roberto Jr., in August 1965. Their second son, Luis Roberto, was born in July 1966.

Now that Roberto spent more time at home, he began a new hobby. He went to beaches near Carolina and collected driftwood. Then he would shape the wood into furniture or gifts for his friends. And he bought an organ for the Clementes' new home and taught himself how to play it.

Roberto Jr. later remembered people coming to their house all day long. They wanted to meet the great Clemente. Roberto would greet each stranger who came to the door, ask how he could help them, and sometimes talk for hours.

However, Vera said, "[When he could,] he avoided other commitments to spend time with his family. There'd be no baseball talk at the house, unless there'd be visitors who'd begin asking questions."

Back in Pittsburgh with the Pirates, he tried to stay healthy. He made a drink out of raw eggs, sugar, and fruit juice to give him strength.

And he had a spoonful of honey before each game. But he still battled a series of small injuries to his back, legs, elbow, and shoulder.

In 1966, Roberto finally earned the National League Most Valuable Player Award. "It's the highest honor a player can hope for," he said. "Of course, it could have gone to Sandy Koufax, but I had the best season of my career and I was confident the sports writers would vote for me. I am thankful they did."

In 1967, he won his fourth N.L. batting championship with a .357 average, the highest of his career. Roberto is still one of only eight players ever to win that many N.L. batting titles. Despite his growing fame, Roberto answered his fan mail regularly. He always sorted it so that first he would answer the letters from children in cities where the Pirates would be playing next. And he often visited children in hospitals as the team made its way around the country.

He once said that he signed more than twenty thousand autographs a year.

At home, he wanted to use his fame and money to build a huge sports park in Puerto Rico. On one large site, he planned to construct sports fields, gyms, and classrooms. Children from around the island could come there to learn new sports and improve their skills. He found land for this project and started raising money to buy it and build his dream. In 1969, he and Vera were delighted when their third son, Enrique, was born.

He continued to work with many young players from Latin America who were arriving in the United States to play in the majors. The success of Roberto and other players from the Caribbean led the Major League Baseball teams to scout for and hire more Caribbean ballplayers. Roberto made sure to meet with the new players as he traveled from city to city. He would take them out to dinner or give them advice about how to adjust to life in the United States and the big leagues.

LATIN AMERICAN BALLPLAYERS

ONLY A HANDFUL OF PLAYERS FROM THE CARIBBEAN PLAYED IN THE MAJORS BEFORE ROBERTO CLEMENTE. SEVERAL CUBAN PLAYERS REACHED THE UNITED STATES IN THE EARLY TWENTIETH CENTURY. A FEW PLAYERS FROM THE DOMINICAN REPUBLIC AND PUERTO RICO PLAYED IN THE 1950S AS WELL. WITH THE SUCCESS OF ROBERTO AND OTHERS IN THE 1960S, HOWEVER, THE NUMBERS GREW QUICKLY. BY THE 1970S, DOZENS OF PLAYERS FROM MANY LATIN AMERICAN COUNTRIES HAD BEEN RECRUITED TO PLAY MAJOR LEAGUE BALL.

IN 2009, A PERMANENT EXHIBIT OPENED AT THE BASEBALL HALL OF FAME IN COOPERSTOWN, NEW YORK. "¡VIVA BASEBALL!" CELEBRATES THE MANY STAR PLAYERS WHO HAD COME FROM CARIBBEAN AND LATIN AMERICAN COUNTRIES.

IN ADDITION TO ROBERTO, SOME OTHER GREAT LATIN AMERICAN BASEBALL PLAYERS ARE:

- TONY PÉREZ AND TONY OLIVA (CUBA)
- ROD CAREW AND MARIANO RIVERA (PANAMA)
- JUAN MARICHAL, PEDRO MARTÍNEZ, ALBERT PUJOLS, AND ROBINSON CANÓ (DOMINICAN REPUBLIC)
- IVÁN RODRÍGUEZ AND ROBERTO ALOMAR (PUERTO RICO)

AS OF 2013, MORE THAN 27 PERCENT OF
PLAYERS IN THE MAJOR LEAGUES WERE FROM
SPANISH-SPEAKING COUNTRIES.

Chapter 9
Back to the Top

By 1970, Roberto's many good deeds had become well-known. On July 24, the Pirates honored him with a special ceremony at their home ballpark in Pittsburgh.

Dozens of friends and family flew up from Puerto Rico for Roberto Clemente Night. Even Melchor came up with Luisa, finally overcoming his fear of flying. His wife and sons looked on proudly. Speeches were made in Spanish and English, honoring and thanking Roberto. Roberto asked people donate money to a Pittsburgh children's hospital, rather than to honor him with gifts.

In early 1971, at a banquet in Houston, Roberto was given the Tris Speaker Memorial Award as top player by the Baseball Writers Association of America. They were among the same people who had insulted him in the past, the same men who had once made fun of his accent.

This time, they chose him for his achievements on and off the field. By speaking out against racism, by always encouraging Puerto Ricans, and by giving time and money to make others' lives better, Roberto had become more than just a ballplayer. The writers had finally recognized that.

In a speech accepting the award, he said these memorable words about his life and his goals: "If you have a chance to accomplish something that will make things better for people coming behind you, and you don't do that, you are wasting your time on this earth."

❖ ❖ ❖

The 1971 season was another triumph for the Pirates and for Roberto. That year, the Pirates won the N.L. East Division in the regular season. That sent them to the playoffs, where they beat the San Francisco Giants. That victory gave Pittsburgh a matchup against the Baltimore Orioles in the World Series.

Just to reach the first game of the World Series, however, Roberto had to rally himself one more time. While in Baltimore before the first game, he became very ill with food poisoning. "The doctor was worried and I was worried," said Vera. "He didn't sleep at all, but he went to the game and played well."

He did better than that—he dominated.

Roberto had a hit in every one of the seven games. He played perfect defense. His home run in game seven put the Pirates in the lead for good.

After hitting .414 in the World Series, he was named the World Series Most Valuable Player. Roberto was now the game's biggest star. Along with the joy of Roberto Clemente Night a year earlier, this World Series was the high point of Roberto's career.

He received his award amid the celebration in the clubhouse. While being interviewed on live television, Roberto spoke from his heart. And he did so in Spanish, which had never been done during a Major League Baseball broadcast on live TV before. He spoke to the people he loved most, his family. *"En el día más grande de mi vida, para los nenes la bendición mía y que mis padres me echen la bendición."* ("In this most important day of my life, I give blessings to my boys and ask that my parents give their blessing.")

A year later, as he was considering retiring from baseball, Roberto got his three thousandth hit. In 1972, he was only the eleventh player to reach that mark. He was the first Hispanic player with three thousand hits. The Pirates made the playoffs again in the 1972 season, but lost the N.L. championship series to the Cincinnati Reds. Roberto, as he did after every season, said good-bye to his teammates and went back to Puerto Rico. They did not know they would never see him again.

Chapter 10
A Sudden End

In November 1972,
Roberto was named
the manager of an
all-star team from
Puerto Rico.
They traveled to
Nicaragua to play
in a tournament.
During his weeks
there, Roberto did
what he always
did—he led baseball clinics

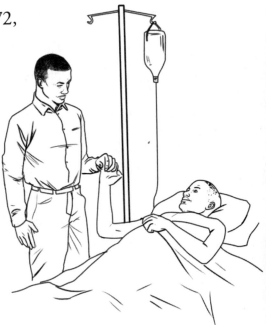

and he visited sick children in hospitals. He met
one young man with injured legs and promised to
help pay for his surgery. Every morning, he took a

bag of coins and went out in the streets and passed out the money. Roberto grew very close to the Nicaraguan people in his short visit.

Before he returned home, he brought a pet spider monkey for Ricky, toys for his other children, and new clothes for Vera. He had many presents for his parents and other relatives.

In late December, a terrible earthquake struck Nicaragua. Many of the people Roberto had just met were killed or injured. Five square miles at the center of the city of Managua were destroyed. Roberto immediately started to help. He organized a drive to raise money and gather needed supplies such as food, medicine, and clothing. He went on TV and radio and urged people to give money and support to the earthquake victims.

Soon a plane was making flights from Puerto Rico to Nicaragua.

Not long after the supplies began arriving in Nicaragua, Roberto heard they were being misused and not always given to those who needed them most. He was shocked, but he knew what he had to do. He would go himself to make sure that the people, his friends, got what they needed.

As he was getting ready to leave for Nicaragua, he found that there was too much to carry in one plane. To take all the supplies that people had donated, Roberto hired a second plane. He did not know that this second plane had recently been in a crash. He did not know that most of the crew had little experience flying this kind of large aircraft. He did not know that they overloaded the plane by thousands of pounds. He only wanted to help.

Just after 9:00 p.m. on New Year's Eve, the plane carrying Roberto and the relief supplies lumbered down the runway in San Juan. The aircraft slowly rose, but just barely cleared the trees at the end of the runway. A moment later, one engine made a loud bang. The pilot tried to turn around, but it was too late. The airplane was over the ocean. It could not turn back. The airplane crashed into the sea.

As word got out, thousands of people rushed to the beach near the crash site. Divers went into the water, boats looked for survivors and wreckage. They searched for days. Almost nothing was ever found. The entire island and the baseball world started the new year—1973—with sad and shocking news. Roberto Clemente was dead at the age of thirty-eight.

Chapter 11
His Legacy Today

All of baseball was stunned by Roberto's death. His family could not believe it. But they were all proud of what people said about Roberto. Letters and notes poured in from all over. Teammates and other friends flew from Pittsburgh to Puerto Rico for a funeral Mass. Eventually, money raised in his name would help build a children's wing for a hospital in Nicaragua.

Just a few days after he died, the Baseball Hall of Fame announced that he could be voted in right away. Normally, a player must wait five years after his career ends to earn this honor. But after the voting was over, Roberto was named to the Hall of Fame in March 1973. It was only the second time that the baseball writers, who vote for the Hall of Fame, had done this for a player. (The first was for Yankees first baseman Lou Gehrig, in 1939.)

Also that year, Major League Baseball created the Roberto Clemente Award. It is given each season to a player who continues Roberto's legacy. The winning player must excel on the field and be a great help to his community and to the world.

The US government honored Roberto as well. President Richard Nixon was one of the first to personally donate money to help build Roberto's longed-for sports center in Puerto Rico. In May 1973, Nixon gave the first Presidential Citizens Medal to Roberto. Vera traveled to the White House to accept the honor. "I think he would be proud to be the first American to get this medal," she said.

In 1974, Ciudad Deportiva Roberto Clemente (Roberto Clemente Sports City) opened in Carolina. Vera went on to run the site for decades. "When he died, I felt the responsibility to make a reality of a sports city," Vera Clemente said. "My main purpose was to do what he was planning to do." Roberto Clemente Sports City still attracts thousands of young people year-round for baseball and many other activities.

The honors for Roberto continued long after his death. In 1998, a bridge in Pittsburgh near the Pirates' new ballpark was renamed in his honor.

ROBERTO CLEMENTE AWARD

THE ROBERTO CLEMENTE AWARD IS ONE OF THE BIGGEST HONORS A MAJOR LEAGUE PLAYER CAN RECEIVE. IT IS PRESENTED DURING THE WORLD SERIES IN A SPECIAL CEREMONY TO A PLAYER WHO DEMONSTRATES A COMMITMENT BOTH TO THE GAME OF BASEBALL AND TO HELPING HIS COMMUNITY.

HERE ARE JUST A FEW OF THE SUPERSTARS WHO HAVE EARNED THIS HONOR:

2011	DAVID ORTIZ, BOSTON RED SOX
2009	DEREK JETER, NEW YORK YANKEES
2008	ALBERT PUJOLS, ST. LOUIS CARDINALS
1999	TONY GWYNN, SAN DIEGO PADRES
1992	CAL RIPKEN JR., BALTIMORE ORIOLES
1988	DALE MURPHY, ATLANTA BRAVES
1977	ROD CAREW, MINNESOTA TWINS

In 2003, President George W. Bush gave Vera, on Roberto's behalf, the Presidential Medal of Freedom. In 2012, the professional league in Puerto Rico where Roberto got his start renamed itself. Current players follow in his footsteps in the Liga de Béisbol Profesional Roberto Clemente.

Today, decades after Roberto Clemente's death, thousands of young men from the Caribbean have seen their baseball dreams come true in the minor and major leagues. Roberto was not the first Latin American ballplayer to make it, but he was the best. He led by example. His hard work, courage, and generosity continue to impact Puerto Rico, baseball, and the world.

TIMELINE OF
ROBERTO CLEMENTE'S LIFE

1934	Roberto Clemente born in Puerto Rico
1954	Signed by Brooklyn Dodgers; plays season in Montreal
1955	Drafted by Pittsburgh Pirates; plays first Major League Baseball season
1960	Wins World Series with Pirates
1961	Wins first of four National League batting titles and first of twelve Gold Gloves
1964	Marries Vera Zabala
1965	Son Roberto Jr. born
1966	Son Luis born Wins N.L. MVP award
1969	Son Enrique born
1970	Roberto Clemente Night held in Pittsburgh
1971	Wins second World Series; named World Series MVP
1972	Gets three thousandth career hit Killed in plane crash while delivering relief supplies to Nicaragua Elected to the Baseball Hall of Fame
1973	Vera receives the first Presidential Citizen's Medal on behalf of Roberto from President Richard Nixon
2003	Vera receives the Presidential Medal of Freedom on behalf of Roberto from President George W. Bush

TIMELINE OF THE WORLD

World War II ends — **1945**

Puerto Rico becomes a commonwealth of the United States — **1952**

A Communist revolution in Cuba puts Fidel Castro in charge — **1959**

John F. Kennedy is elected president of the United States — **1960**

Yuri Gagarin of the Soviet Union is the first man in space — **1961**

The Cuban Missile Crisis affects the US and the Soviet Union — **1962**

The March on Washington increases focus on civil rights movement
President Kennedy is assassinated in Dallas — **1963**

The Beatles perform on US television for the first time
US Congress passes the Civil Rights Act — **1964**

The first Super Bowl is played — **1967**

Martin Luther King Jr. is killed in Memphis — **1968**

Apollo 11 lands the first men on the moon — **1969**

Richard Nixon becomes first US president to resign office — **1974**

America celebrates its bicentennial (two hundredth birthday) — **1976**

BIBLIOGRAPHY

* Buckley, James Jr. **Roberto Clemente**. New York: DK Publishing, 2001.

Clemente Family. **Clemente: The True Legacy of an Undying Hero**. New York: Celebra, 2013.

Maraniss, David. **Clemente: The Passion and Grace of Baseball's Last Hero**. New York: Simon & Schuster, 2006.

Markusen, Bruce. **Roberto Clemente: The Great One**. Champaign, IL: Sports Publishing, 1998.

Musick, Phil. **Who Was Roberto?: A Biography of Roberto Clemente**. New York: Doubleday, 1974.

* Santiago, Wilfred. **21: The Story of Roberto Clement: A Graphic Novel**. Seattle: Fantagraphics, 2011.

* Winter, Jonah. **Roberto Clemente: Pride of the Pittsburgh Pirates**. New York: Atheneum Books for Young Readers, 2005.

* Books for young readers